T0039968

HILARY McHONE

Jenny Schwartz

God's Ear

JENNY SCHWARTZ's play *God's Ear* was produced by New Georges in May 2007 and was produced again off-Broadway in the spring of 2008 by the Vineyard Theatre in association with New Georges. Jenny's play-in-progress, *Somewhere Fun*, was first developed at Soho Rep's Writer/Director Lab and is now under co-commission between Soho Rep and Soho Theatre, London, where Jenny spent a month as a playwright-in-residence. Two of Jenny's plays, *Intervals* and *Cause for Alarm*, were part of the New York International Fringe Festival, in 1998 and 2002, respectively. She is the recipient of a grant from the Lincoln Center Lecomte du Nuoy Foundation and is the 2007–2008 recipient of the Dorothy Strelsin Foundation Fellowship at Soho Rep. An associate artist with the Civilians and a board member of New Georges, Jenny completed two years of fellowship in the Playwriting Program at the Juilliard School and holds an MFA in theatre directing from Columbia University.

God's Ear

God's
Ear

Jenny
Schwartz

FARRAR, STRAUS AND GIROUX

NEW YORK

Farrar, Strauss & Giroux
18 West 18th Street, New York 10011

Printed in the United States of America
First edition, 2008

Library of Congress Cataloging-in-Publication Data
Schwartz, Jenny, 1973–
    God's ear / Jenny Schwartz.— 1st ed.
        p.   cm.
    ISBN-13: 978-0-86547-990-6 (pbk. : alk. paper)
    ISBN-10: 0-86547-990-9 (pbk. : alk. paper)
    1. Children—Death—Drama.   2. Grief—Drama.   3. Loss (Psychology)—
Drama.   I. Title.

PS3619.C4868 G63 2008
812'.6—dc22

                                                        2007037476

Designed by Gretchen Achilles

www.fsgbooks.com

P1

For Margaret, Candace, and Peg

Acknowledgments

The playwright wishes to thank

Aaron Stone 💙

as well as many others
including but nowhere near limited to

Sarah Stern
Ken Rus Schmoll
Mark Christian Subias
Susan Bernfield and New Georges
Doug Aibel and the Vineyard Theatre
Chris D., Marsha N., Joe K.
and the Juilliard School Drama Division
Denise Oswald
Nina Steiger
Michael Friedman
The ever-so-talented casts, designers, crews, and staffs
of all readings, workshops, and productions
especially Christina, Gibson, Annie Mac,
Monique, Raymond, Matt, and Judith
not to mention Kris, Tyler, Leah, Olivera, and Megan
Celia Gerard
Phoebe Hope Stone ☺

and

Anne Kauffman

The Shadow of a Future Self

by Nina Steiger

Jenny Schwartz uses language like a composer might, embellishing a simple melody with harmonics. Harmonic pitches, made up of partial or component frequencies, are what give different instruments their distinct timbres and give us the ability to determine that two instruments playing in unison are in fact distinct from each other. The range of sounds an instrument is capable of is amplified and what we can hear is extended by these "partials." As a composer might use these tones to complexify a melody, likewise, Jenny's characters, scenes, and moments—fragments and partials themselves—are able to convey an expansive and nuanced emotional landscape using deceptively simple elements.

When I first talked to Jenny about her process, she indicated that it could be a time-consuming one, working toward "getting it right." But it wasn't until we worked together on a script-in-progress for Soho Theatre that I truly appreciated the precision with which she forges the kind of moments that distinguish her work. She massages the rhythms and beats of each scene with an alertness to the intentions underneath each line. She has astonishing instincts for capturing the hidden languages we speak when we talk casually to the people we treasure most and intimately with those we don't know at all.

Jenny's scenes are characterized by people in apparent isolation. They seem to find it easy to talk, but hard to say what they mean; simple to express something, but never in their own words. This creates a particular and often peculiar rhythm and vernacular. Her characters seem to invite us into the recesses of their marriages, their memories, and their dramas with the most familiar of phrases. Yet these phrases are applied in new ways, overturned and contraverted to let us know that there is more to what's said than what we hear. "I have deficiencies," Mel tells Ted. Repetitions are woven into the dialogue. At the heart of this is the accrued meaning a phrase or confrontation gains in repeated approaches, each time affording the characters a higher sense of emotional acuity and the audience a deeper sense of identification.

Like an antenna capturing multiple frequencies, Jenny pinpoints lives comprised of fragments—echoes of memory and dreams, conversations we're too busy to finish, snippets we hear from other peoples' cell-phone calls, moments we observe in waiting rooms, lounges, and lobbies. The comparison to harmonics lies in Jenny's masterful use of partial thoughts and moments that combine to give her work its distinct flavor. Her writing captures something of the pain and humor within a particular dissociation so many of us feel today.

These characters have borrowed words from the surrounding atmosphere and have anguish they cannot express. One of the most stirring moments must surely be a long speech of Mel's which becomes an aria of clichés. It begins as a call to arms, a manifesto of newly made meanings and, by extension, possibilities. This speech ends with a reiteration of the marriage vows that are straining in the wake of a loss. We end with a maudlin couplet: "And the fat lady will sing. / With bells on."

The play presents a mosaic; each of its tiles offer grace notes of misunderstanding, odd applications of everyday idioms, overturned clichés, and phantom lines from one character in the mouth of another. What emerges from the fragments is a compelling portrait of grief and recalibration. It's a perfect snapshot of a family in transition and it articulates aspects of the human heart and the modern condition. "We am. / I. / Were. / We was."

Nina Steiger is the director of the Writers' Centre
at Soho Theatre, London.

God's Ear

Production History

God's Ear was developed at the Juilliard School and the Vineyard Theatre, New York City.

God's Ear had its world premiere in a New Georges (Susan Bernfield, Artistic Director; Sarah Cameron Sunde, Associate Director) production at the East Thirteenth Street Theatre in New York City on May 2, 2007. Director: Anne Kauffman. Songs by Michael Friedman with additional lyrics by Jenny Schwartz. Dramaturg: Sarah Stern. Set Designer: Kris Stone. Lighting Designer: Tyler Micoleau. Sound Designer: Leah Gelpe. Costume Designer: Olivera Gajic. Casting: Paul Davis/Calleri Casting. Assistant Director: Maryna Harrison. Production Stage Manager: Megan Schwarz. Assistant Stage Manager: Danielle Teague-Daniels. Production Management: Samuel C. Tresler, Hilary McHone.

MEL   *Christina Kirk*

TED   *Gibson Frazier*

LANIE   *Monique Vukovic*

THE TOOTH FAIRY   *Judith Greentree*

LENORA   *Annie McNamara*

FLIGHT ATTENDANT / GI JOE   *Matthew Montelongo*

GUY   *Raymond McAnally*

God's Ear was subsequently produced by the Vineyard Theatre, in association with New Georges, in New York City and opened on April 17, 2008. Vineyard Theatre: Douglas Aibel, Aristic Director; Jennifer Garvey-Blackwell, Executive Director; Sarah Stern, Associate Artistic Director; Reed Ridgley, General Manager; Ben Morris, Production Manager. The creative team and the cast remained the same except for the role of Lenora, which was played by Rebecca Wisocky.

Characters

MEL

TED, *Mel's husband*

LANIE, *Mel and Ted's six-year-old daughter*

THE TOOTH FAIRY

LENORA, *a lady at a lounge*

FLIGHT ATTENDANT

GUY, *a guy at a bar*

GI JOE

Note: GI JOE and FLIGHT ATTENDANT are played by the same actor.

Notes on the Text

- The play is divided up into scenes, acts, and interludes to provide clarity for the reader. However, in performance, the play functions as one continuous event.

- Certain songs are labeled as interludes between scenes, while other songs are part of the action of a particular scene. The interlude songs must also affect the action and contribute to the momentum of the play as a whole.

- Once a character has entered the stage, he or she does not necessarily have to exit, unless it is specified in the text. THE TOOTH FAIRY, for example, may stay on stage throughout the entire production. Even so, every effort should be made to direct the audience's attention to the scene at hand.

- Hopefully, the audience will acquire meaning from the accumulation of the language. So, for the most part and unless otherwise noted, actors should speak fast and think on the line.

Prologue

A hospital.

MEL
He's in a coma.
He's hooked up to a respirator.
He has a pulse.
He has brain damage.
Due to lack of . . .
Extensive brain damage.
Due to lack of . . .

His pupils are unreactive,
they said.
He doesn't withdraw from pain,
they said.
The next twenty-four hours are critical.

Or was it crucial?
Or was it critical?
Or was it crucial?

He's in critical condition,
they said.
Survival.
They said.
His chances of survival.
They said,
low.

They said,
the next twenty-four hours are crucial to his chances of
    survival,

they said,
lost.

They said,
his reflexes are—
lost.

What do you mean he has a pulse?
I said.
Of course he has a pulse,
I said.

They're doing all they can,
they said.
Helping him to breathe.
Providing him with—

TED
Oxygen?

MEL
Fluids.
Electrolytes.
Nutrients.
They said.

Most children,
they said,
most children who do survive this extent of a near drowning,
extent of a,
most children,
they said,
are unable to walk and unable to talk,
and most children—

TED
Our son isn't like most children.

Jenny Schwartz

MEL
That's what I told them.
That's exactly what I told them.
I told them our son isn't like most children.

He's not.
Is he?

TED
I don't think so.

MEL
I don't think so either.

Unlikely,
they said,
recovery is unlikely.
They said,
poor.
They said.
Prognosis is—
poor.

TED
Did you tell them to go to hell?
I would have told them to go to hell.

MEL
I told them,
take my reflexes,
I told them,
give him my reflexes,
I told them.

TED
They didn't say anything about miracles, did they?

MEL
Miracles?
No.
Not that I recall.

TED
Hope?

MEL
What about hope?

TED
Did they happen to mention hope?

MEL
They asked us to consider organ donation.

Gentle,
they were,
gentle,
with a,
hand on my shoulder,
they were,
gentle.

What's the definition of prognosis?
Exactly.
I know, but I don't know.

TED
I *don't* know, but I know.

MEL
I told them,
take my brain stem,
I told them,
give him my brain stem,
I told them.

TED
I'm here.

MEL
No,
but thank you,
I told them.
I do not deserve gentle.
I told them.

Interlude: Lanie sings a song.

LANIE
You can't see the cars on the street today.
Only mounds of snow.

No cars.
No cars.
Today.
Only snow.

You don't see people at all.
Today.
You don't see any people at all.

Sometimes in the winter, you will catch yourself in the mirror,
     and you will know what you will look like when you are old.
When you are old.

You can't go anywhere at all.
Because all the cars are buried.

Pretend all the cars are buried.
Pretend all the cars in the world are buried.

Act 1

Scene 1

MEL *and* LANIE *are at home.* TED *comes and goes.*

MEL
Are you my husband?
I can't tell.
It's dark in here.
And I'm floating around.
And my mind is empty.
And my body is empty.
And my soul . . .
Do I *have* a soul?
How was your flight?

TED
Fine.
I slept.

MEL
Did you sleep?

TED
Off and on.

MEL
The whole time?

TED
Almost.

MEL
Good.
You needed it.
Did you take a pill?

TED
I did.

MEL
One or two?

TED
Just one.

MEL
One and a half?

TED
Just one.

MEL
Three?

TED
One.

MEL
Good.

TED
Three are two too many.

MEL
I know.
Are you mocking me?
You're mocking me.
Did you eat?

TED
A little.

MEL
Are you hungry?

TED
Starving.

MEL
Don't say starving.
I'm trying to get Lanie to stop saying she's starving.
She's not starving.
She gets a hundred percent of her daily everything.
Should I fix you something when you get home?
I could make my famous omelet.
Although I'd rather not break any legs.

TED
Eggs?

MEL
Danger: salmonella.
Let me know what you decide.

TED
How is Lanie?

MEL
Fine, she's fine.
She wants to be Helen Keller when she grows up.
I don't know what to tell her.

TED
And you?

MEL
I'd like to own my own shop.

Flowers.
Maybe.
No . . . convenience.
No . . . concessions.
Ted?

TED
Yes?

MEL
Remember that pillbox?
The one I got you?
The organizer?
With the days of the week?
I looked for it.
I couldn't find it.
Will you look for it?
For me?
Please?
When you get home?
I went to the doctor.
He says I'm deficient.
I have deficiencies.
He gave me a list.
A list of vitamins.
Have you heard of boron?
Selenium?
Vitamin B-12?
Vitamin C-3PO?
I went to the drugstore.
I bought some for you too.
Men's vitamins.
You'll find them in the kitchen, on the counter, next to the tea.
I moved the tea.
I took the tea bags out of their boxes and put them in jars,
    glass jars, in the kitchen, on the counter, next to the
    vitamins.
I cleaned out the medicine cabinet.

Jenny Schwartz

I cleaned it up.

I cleaned it out and up.

There was a bottle of cough medicine stuck to the shelf.

I couldn't get it off.

I chipped away at it.

With a knife.

Finally, it gave.

But then, it slipped and shattered, and I must have screamed,
because Lanie came running, and she was screaming too,
and I said, "Don't come in here, Lanie, not with bare feet."

And she said, "What about the dog?"

And I said, "What about the cat?"

And she said, "What about the bunny?"

And I said, "We don't have a bunny."

And she said, "Please can we get a bunny, please please please?"

And I said, "Bunnies aren't domestic."

And she said, "Neither are you."

And I said, "Some things are better left outside."

But then, it wasn't blood at all.

Only cough medicine.

From 1903.

Oh and Ted, the closet in the hallway, with the full-length
mirror, I went to open the door, and the doorknob came
out.

There I was with a doorknob in my hand.

There I was with a doorknob in my hand.

There's an echo.

Do you hear it?

There's an echo.

Do you hear it?

I tried to shove it back in, but it wouldn't catch.

Would you mind prying it open for me, please, the closet door,
when you get home, if you don't mind?

Thanks.

Or else I'll have to go out and buy all new everything.

And I don't want to do that.

I'm ill-equipped.

TED
How are you otherwise?

MEL
The same.
Pretty much.

TED
More or less?

MEL
More.

TED
Give or take?

MEL
Take.

TED
Damn it!
I cut my ear.
Earlier.
I was shaving.

MEL
I bit my lip.
Before.
I also burned my tongue.
And my urine, Ted, it's blue, baby blue.
Not to worry, though, I called the doctor, and it's normal to be
    deficient.
How was your flight?

TED
Pain in the neck.
The woman sitting next to me on the plane, she looked so
    familiar.

MEL
Was she an actress?

TED
I don't think so.

MEL
A movie star?

TED
I don't know.

MEL
Next time have her sign something.
Have her sign your ticket.
Was she a news anchor?

TED
She asked me what I did to my ear.

MEL
Why do they call themselves anchors?

TED
I told her I cut it shaving.
She ordered five vodkas.
I said, "Who orders five vodkas?"
She said, "Who shaves their ear?"
Anyway, we got to talking, and what do you know . . .

MEL
Why is it that everyone you talk to has a dead son?

TED
Small world?

MEL
Tiny.

TED
Life is short?

MEL
Life is a shrimp.

TED
He was ten, she said.
He drowned.
She was looking the other way.

MEL
On the plane?

TED
Never mind.

MEL
At the lake?

TED
What lake?

MEL
And my feet are pale.
And I've lost my slippers.
And the cat has chlamydia.
Again.

TED
Not again.

MEL
And the dog bit the electrician.
His upper, inner thigh.
It's too bad because I liked the electrician.
Ruddy cheeks.
He was Irish.

He was here every day for seven days, and on the seventh day,
    she bit him.
And now he's gone, and look at me, I can't see a thing.
Where are you now?

TED
Baggage claim.

MEL
What are you doing?

TED
Waiting for my bag.

MEL
I thought you hate checking bags.
I thought as long as you live, you'll never check another one.

TED
I was early.
I had time to kill.
I didn't want to lug it around.

MEL
Did you go to duty free?
Did you buy me my perfume?
I'm out.
I'm almost out.

TED
I did.
I tried.
There was a line.

MEL
Did you forget?

TED
I never forget.

MEL
You were early.
You could have waited.

TED
I was starving.
I had to eat.

MEL
Don't say starving.
I'm trying to get Lanie to stop saying she's starving.
She's not starving.
She gets a hundred percent of her daily everything.
Should I fix you something when you get home?
I could make my famous omelet.
Although I'd rather not break any legs.

TED
Eggs?

MEL
Danger: salmonella.
Let me know what you decide.

TED
How is Lanie?

MEL
Fine, she's fine.
You'll never guess . . .
She lost a tooth.

TED
Which one?

MEL
The loose one.

TED
Which one?

MEL
This one.
Here.
She was eating popcorn.
Unpopped.
Just the kernels.
I have the tooth fairy here.
We're waiting for you.
Are you almost home?
Or should we go ahead without you?

TED
I'm on the bridge.

MEL
You should avoid the bridge.

THE TOOTH FAIRY *appears.*

Remember when I looked in the mirror and caught your eye,
    and all of a sudden, we were together again?
And then you went away.
And I was somewhere else.
We'd call and check in.
At first, every day.
Then, less so, over time.
I wrote you a letter.
Did you get it?
Did I mail it?
Dear Ted,
Are you my husband?
I can't tell.

You have the silhouette of my husband.
But silhouettes can be deceiving.
Are you coming home for dinner?
Christmas?
Easter?
Nor'easter?

TED
Maybe.
Maybe not.

MEL
Which is it?
Maybe?
Or maybe not?
Is my guess as good as yours?
Oh and Ted, your sister called.

TED
Which one?

MEL
The loose one.

TED
Which one?

MEL
That one.
There.
I told her you were out.
Exploring other options.
Signed, M.
As in empty.
Smiley face.
P.S. Send this letter to twenty-five people in twenty-five
    minutes and get rich quick.

Otherwise . . . *(makes throat-slitting gesture and sound)*
You're soaking wet.

TED
It's raining.

MEL
Do you want a towel?
I'll get you a towel.

TED
I'm sorry.

MEL
Don't be sorry.

TED
I'm sorry.

MEL
You should be.

TED
I'm sorry.

MEL
You always say that and you always lie.

TED
I'm somewhat sorry.
Does that count?
I lost my umbrella.

MEL
You could have bought a new one.

TED
I wanted to get home.

MEL
I'm glad you're home.

TED
I'm glad I'm home too.
I missed you.

MEL
I missed you too.

TED
No, but I really missed you.
Those are just words to you, but I mean it.

MEL
I mean it too.

TED
Then, tell me again.

MEL
I mean it too.

TED
Damn it!

MEL
You did cut your ear.

TED
Look at you.

MEL
Don't look at my feet.
Take off your clothes.
You're going to catch cold.
Tomorrow, you'll call in sick.
I'll take care of you.

Jenny Schwartz

I don't know how, but I'm sure I'll think of something.
I'll make you chicken soup.
And cinnamon toast.
You can blow your nose in my sleeve.
Remember I used to roll up my sleeve, and you'd tickle my
    arm?
At the movies?
Under the table?
And now, I'd rather cut off my arm than have you tickle it.
Don't go.
Stay.
You're always running off.
How was your flight?

TED
What do you care?

MEL
Come back.

TED
And then what?

MEL
And then you'll say, "Why? Why are you always so mean?"

TED
You used to be so sweet.
You used to say "Gesundheit" to the dog.

MEL
And then we'll kiss.
And then I'll scratch your back.

Higher.
A little higher.
There.
Right there.

And then you'll hold me.
And protect me.
And I'll forgive you.
And you'll understand me.

And I'll never stop loving you.
And you won't ever think of leaving me.
And I'll laugh at all your jokes.
And you'll never disappoint me.

And you'll swoop down and save the day.
And I'll bend over backwards and light up the room.

And we'll thank God.
And God will bless America.
And with God as our witness, we'll never be starving again.

And the fog will lift.
And we'll see eye to eye.
And the cows will come home.
And we'll dance cheek to cheek.

And we'll face the music.
And smell the coffee.
And know where to turn.
And which end is up.

And the dogs will stop biting.
And the bees will stop stinging.
And this too shall pass.
And all good things.

And we'll make love.
The old-fashioned way.
Blindfolded.
With one hand tied behind our back.

Jenny Schwartz

And hell will be freezing.
And pigs will be flying.
And Rome will be built.
And water will be wine.

And truth will be told.
And needs will be met.
And boys will be boys.
And enough will be enough.

And we'll cross that bridge.
And bridge that gap.
And bear that cross.
And cross that *t*.

And part that sea.
And act that part.
And turn that leaf.
And turn that cheek.

And speak our minds.
And mind our manners.
And clear our heads.
And right our wrongs.

And count our blessings.
And count our chickens.
And pick our battles.
And eat our words.

And take it slow.
And make it last.
And have it made.
And make it fast.

And take it back.
And see it through.
And see the light.
And raise the roof.

And make the most.
And make the best.
And work it out.
And mend the fence.

And wait it out.
And play it down.
And live it up.
And paint the town.

And take care.
And eat right.
And sleep well.
And stay calm.

And have fun.
And have faith.
And face facts.
And move on.

And own up.
And come clean.
And start fresh.
And take charge.

And stand tall.
And save face.
And steer clear.
And live large.

And then we'll kick up our heels.
And have it both ways.
And take a deep breath.
And take it like men.

And sit back.
Relax.

And ride off into the horseshit.

For richer, for poorer.
In sickness and in health.
And the fat lady will sing.
With bells on.

THE TOOTH FAIRY *sings to* MEL *and* TED.

THE TOOTH FAIRY

> *The sun is rising on the sea.*
> *My bowl is full of cherries.*
> *The best things in life all are free,*
> *And we believe in fairies.*
>
> *My life is like Act Five, Scene Three,*
> *Where everybody marries.*
> *And if misery loves company,*
> *Why am I standing here all alone?*
>
> *There are rings and rings around the moon.*
> *The clouds have silver linings.*
> *I gather all the teeth at noon,*
> *And take them to book signings.*
> *I'm whistling a happy tune,*
> *And drinking tea from Twinings.*

And if nothing interesting happens soon,
I'm gonna—(makes throat-slitting gesture and sound)

You have no idea what it means to be a public figure.

I'm not usually this heavy.
But I recently had a baby.
Unfortunately—

TED
Did he die?

THE TOOTH FAIRY
He did.

TED
Anything I can do?

THE TOOTH FAIRY
You can hand me a tissue.
With aloe.
Aloe is nature's way of saying I'm sorry.

TED
Sorry?

THE TOOTH FAIRY
Nothing.

TED
What?

THE TOOTH FAIRY
Forget it.

TED
Sorry?

Jenny Schwartz

THE TOOTH FAIRY
Nothing.

TED
What?

MEL
Ow!
Paper cut.
I'm bleeding.

TED
Are you bleeding?

MEL
It's deep.

TED
Is it deep?

MEL
Quiet.
It's healing.
A scab.

TED
Don't pick it.

MEL
I'll pick it if I want to.
It's my scab, isn't it?

TED
I paid for it, didn't I?

MEL
I took a bath, then cleaned the tub, then took a bath, then
    cleaned the tub.

I made a list, then ripped it up, then made a list, then ripped
it up.
I bought a new fish for the fish tank.
But it killed all the other fish, and then it killed itself.

TED
How are you otherwise?

MEL
I'm not all I'm cracked up to be.

TED
I don't know what that means.

MEL
Don't sell yourself short.

TED
I brought you something.

MEL
You shouldn't have.

TED
I wanted to.

MEL
Why?

TED
No reason.

MEL
You know I hate surprises.

TED
Why?

MEL
No reason.

TED
Now, close your eyes.

MEL
For what?

TED
For fun.
Now, open your eyes.

MEL
For what?

TED
For fun.

MEL *(looking at the gift)*
Oh Ted, they're . . .

TED
Slippers.

MEL
Do they keep on giving?

TED
What do you think?

MEL
I love them, I think.
But I don't like them, I don't think.
I like the idea of them, I think.
But I don't like the expression of the idea of them, I don't
    think.

TED

I saw them in the store window, and I thought of you.
I thought they looked like you.
Like the way you used to look.
Before you bit your tongue.

MEL

Lip.

TED

Before you burned your tongue.
I can't talk.
I'm in a room full of people.
It's hot.
We're sweating through our suits.

MEL

And the women?

TED

There are no women.

MEL

And the hotel?

TED

It's all right.

MEL

How's your room?

TED

I suppose.

MEL

Wait.

TED
What?

MEL
Shh . . .
I'm trying to imagine the rest of my life without you . . .
Ted?

TED
Yes?

MEL
What's that around your ankle?
Is that a thong?
Is that a thong around your ankle?
Why is there a thong around your ankle?
Who does it belong to?
No don't tell me please don't tell me no don't tell me I don't
    want to know.

TED
Amanda.
It belongs to Amanda.

MEL
Does Amanda have a name?

TED
Tina.

MEL
Does Bridget have a name?

TED
Marie.

MEL
Does Chloe have a name?

TED
Sonya.

MEL
Does Hilary have a name?

TED
Gail.

MEL
Does Ellen have a name?

TED
Nancy.

MEL
Does Barbara have a name?

TED
Lourdes.

MEL
Does Ingrid have a name?

TED
Lenora.

MEL
I only know one Lenora.
The electrician, this morning, he gave the dog the finger.
There's a child in this house, I said.
We don't use that finger.

TED
How is the dog?

MEL
Ask her yourself.

TED
How is the dog?

MEL
She doesn't exist as far as the cat's concerned.

TED
How is the dog?

MEL
Needy.
She thinks I'm going to leave her.
I can't imagine why.

TED
How is the dog?

MEL
Clever.
She thinks you get Lyme disease from limes.

TED
How is the dog?

MEL
Bloated.
She thinks food is love and love is food and love is food and
    food is love.

TED
How is the dog?

MEL
She has a feeling we're not in Kansas anymore.

TED
How is the dog?

MEL
Pissy.
She's given up caffeine.
She's gone cold turkey.

TED
And you?

MEL
I turned on the TV and lit a cigarette.

TED
Just one?

MEL
Yes.

TED
Two?

MEL
Yes.

TED
Six?

MEL
Yes.

TED
Ten?

MEL
Did you go to duty free?
Did you buy cigarettes?

TED
I did.
I tried.
There was a line.

MEL
Did you forget?

TED
I never forget.

MEL
You were early.
You could have waited.

TED
I was starving—

MEL
GO AHEAD!
STARVE!
SEE IF I CARE!
SEE IF I NOTICE THAT YOU'RE GONE!
SEE IF I WONDER IF YOU'RE EVER COMING BACK!
ARE YOU EVER COMING BACK?
SEE IF I CARE!
SEE IF I NOTICE THAT YOU'RE GONE!
There's an echo.
Do you hear it?
There's an echo.
Do you hear it?
SEE IF I CARE!
SEE IF I NOTICE THAT YOU'RE GONE!

He kisses her.

TED

I kissed you this morning, but you didn't wake up.
Like that.
But with more tenderness.
If you can imagine more tenderness.

MEL

Was I dreaming?

TED

I don't know.

MEL

I must have been dreaming.

TED

I don't know.

MEL

Did you ever have that dream?
Where you're falling?
And your organs are suspended?
And there's nowhere to go but down?

TED

You're cold.

MEL

Let's go inside.
I'm cold.

TED

We are inside.

MEL

What about the dog?

TED
What about the cat?

MEL
Danger: chlamydia.
Again.

TED
Not again.

MEL
What about the bunny?

TED
We don't have a bunny.

MEL
Did you ever have that dream?

TED
I'm having it now.
Oh well.

MEL
Oh well what?

TED
I'll call you when I land.

MEL
The man in the shop, he sold me a killer fish.
I still haven't cleaned out the tank.
I can't.
I won't do it.
If it's the last thing I don't do.

TED
I brought you something.

MEL
You shouldn't have.

TED
I wanted to.

MEL
Why?

TED
No reason.

MEL
You know I hate surprises.

TED
Why?

MEL
No reason.

TED
Now, close your eyes.

MEL
For what?

TED
For fun.
Now, open your eyes.

MEL
For what?

TED
For fun.

MEL *(looking at the gift)*
Oh Ted, they're . . .

TED
Milk Duds.

MEL
Do they keep on giving?

TED
In case you forgot the day I fell in love with you.

MEL
You know I have a weakness for anything sweet . . .
Lenora from high school.
She was the star of all the plays.
Is your Lenora the star of all the plays?

LANIE *appears.*

LANIE
Look, Ma!
No hands!

TED *(to* MEL*)*
Sit down.

MEL *(to* TED*)*
Tell me.

TED
Sit down.

MEL
Tell me.

Interlude: Lenora sings a song.

LENORA

At the airport,
At the airport last week,
At the airport the other day, I saw a man I thought I knew,
I thought that I'd been introduced to at a party.
I was about to say, "Hello.
Aren't you someone I know?"
But I couldn't remember if his name was Stan or Sid or Marty.
And I thought he might not remember me at all.
I think he'd said that he was going to call.
I haven't seen him since.
This is the first day of the rest of my diet.
It's nice.
It's nice.
And quiet.
Here.

TED

I came all the way back here and I'll be damned if I can
remember why.

Scene 2

LANIE
Who's that?

MEL
That's Dad.

LANIE
Where?

MEL
Right there.

LANIE
Whose voice is that?

MEL
That's Dad's voice.

LANIE
Which voice?

MEL
Speaking.

LANIE
That's not Dad's voice.

MEL
Shh.
In the morning.

LANIE
That's not my dad's voice.

MEL
We'll talk in the morning.

LANIE
That's not my dad.

MEL
We'll talk loud in the morning.
We'll sing our songs.

LANIE
Where's my dad?

MEL
Stop it.
Go back to bed.

LANIE
Where?

MEL
Go back to bed for Sam.

LANIE
Where is he?

MEL
Go back to bed for Dad.

LANIE
Where's Dad?

MEL
Go back to bed, and Dad will come home.

Jenny Schwartz

LANIE
Is there God?

MEL
Hold my hand.
Squeeze my fingers.

LANIE
Is there heaven?

MEL
I don't know.

LANIE
What will we do when Dad comes home?

MEL
I don't know.

LANIE
What will we do?

MEL
I don't know.

LANIE
Who's sadder?
You or Dad?

MEL
Shh.

LANIE
Who's sadder?
Me or you?

MEL
Shh.

LANIE
Who's sadder?
Me or Dad?

MEL
Shh.

LANIE
Who's sadder?
Me, you, or Dad?

MEL
Shh.
I don't know.
We'll do lots of things.
When Dad comes home.
We'll do lots of things.

LANIE
Like what?

MEL
Like sledding.

LANIE
What does Sam look like?

MEL
Sam is buried.

LANIE
In the ground?

MEL
That's right.

LANIE
Sam is in the ground?

MEL
That's right.

LANIE
What does Sam look like?

MEL
Shh.
In the morning.

LANIE
No, now please.

MEL
Shh.

LANIE
No, now please, right this second or I'll forget.

MEL
When Dad comes home, we'll go sledding in the backyard.
I'll bring the camera.
Dad will pull you around and around and around, and I'll take
    pictures.
We'll stay outside for hours and hours, but we won't feel the
    cold.
And then, when we're tired and hungry, we'll go inside and I'll
    make dinner.
We'll turn on the TV and watch the news.
You'll sit on your stool and be my helper.

LANIE
What will we sing?

MEL
You'll chop vegetables, but you won't chop your fingers.
You'll be very, very careful not to chop your fingers.

LANIE
In the kitchen, what will we sing?

MEL
Promise you'll be careful?

LANIE
Will we sing from *Oklahoma*?

MEL
Promise?

LANIE
Will we sing "Oh, What a Beautiful Morning"?

MEL
I don't know.
I don't know anything.
I don't know anything more than you do.
I know less today than I did yesterday, and tomorrow I'll know
    even less.
Shh.
Sam was beautiful, and Dad's sad, so sad.
Dad misses Sam just like we do.
We miss Sam so much, don't we?

LANIE
And Dad?

MEL
We miss Dad too.

LANIE
And Dad's beautiful?

MEL
And Dad's beautiful too.

LANIE
And me?

MEL
And you're beautiful too.
My beautiful, beautiful girl.

On the night you were born, it was snowing and raining at the
     exact same time.
And it looked like the lake was boiling.

LANIE
Boiling . . .

MEL
And the fog was thick.
Like soup.
And it took forever to get to the hospital.
And then, I pushed and pushed, but you were stuck.
And then, you were in distress.
And then, it was the longest minute of my life.
And then, the doctor said, "Here comes the baby, and it's a
     girl."
The end.

LANIE
You're the saddest, then me, then Dad.

MEL
No.

LANIE
I won't chop my fingers.

MEL
No.

LANIE
You have the prettiest voice in the world.

MEL
No.

LANIE
I'm fair.
Like my father.
That's what everyone always says.
Why?

THE TOOTH FAIRY *reappears.*

THE TOOTH FAIRY
Luck of the draw.

LANIE
Are you fair?

THE TOOTH FAIRY
Do I look fair?

LANIE
Open up.
Say ah.

THE TOOTH FAIRY *(opening her mouth)*
Ah.

LANIE
Fair enough.

Scene 3

An airplane. TED *waits for takeoff.* MEL *and* LANIE *remain onstage, at home.*

TED *(to* MEL *on the phone)*
I have to go.
I have to go now.
Because I do.
I just do.
Because it's time.
Because they made an announcement.
Because there's a transvestite stewardess with a gun to my
    head, and she wants me to hang up the phone.

FLIGHT ATTENDANT *appears and puts a gun to* TED's *head.*

Because I know.
I just know.
Because you can tell.
You just can.
No, I don't think it's sad, not really, no, I don't, not at all.
Because she looks happy, that's why.
She looks content.
She looks like she likes what she does, and how many people
    can you say *that* about?
Right, right, right, right?
Count 'em on one—
I don't know.
How should I know?
Do you want me to ask her?
All right.
I'll ask her.

Excuse me, but my wife, she wants to know, what's your
favorite part of your job?

FLIGHT ATTENDANT
Demonstrations.

TED (*to* MEL)
Did you hear that?

FLIGHT ATTENDANT
I like demonstrations.
And also—

TED (*to* MEL)
Did you hear that?

FLIGHT ATTENDANT
I like answering questions.
I like my uniform.
I like my hips in my uniform.
I like my teeth, in the mirror, in the lavatory.
I don't mind lipstick on my teeth.
I don't mind turbulence.
I like children, babies, even when they scream.
I welcome turbulence, flatulence, pestilence, arrogance, war—

TED (*to* MEL)
Did you hear that?

FLIGHT ATTENDANT
Famine—

TED (*to* MEL)
Did you hear that?

FLIGHT ATTENDANT
Denial, anger, bargaining, depression, acceptance.

TED *(to* MEL*)*
Did you hear that?

FLIGHT ATTENDANT
Passion.
All in a day's work.

TED *(to* FLIGHT ATTENDANT*)*
My wife says lucky you.

FLIGHT ATTENDANT
Your wife doesn't know dick about dick.

FLIGHT ATTENDANT *pistol-whips* TED. TED *collapses.*

MEL *(stepping on an action figure)*
Ow.

LANIE *(to* MEL*)*
What's wrong?

FLIGHT ATTENDANT *(to* TED*)*
Sorry.
I don't make the rules.

MEL *(to* LANIE*)*
I stepped on an action figure.
I stepped on another.
They're everywhere.
Underfoot.
I'm going to take them outside and bury them.

LANIE *(to* MEL*)*
Can I help?

MEL
Help me.

LANIE
Can I help?

MEL
Help me help myself.

TED *(to* FLIGHT ATTENDANT*)*
Am I dead?

FLIGHT ATTENDANT *(to* TED*)*
Stunned.
How do you feel?

TED
I don't.

FLIGHT ATTENDANT
If you did?

TED
Stunned.

FLIGHT ATTENDANT
If you did?

TED
Nostalgic.

FLIGHT ATTENDANT
If you did?

TED
Like a shadow of my former self.
Future self.
Former self.
Future self.

Jenny Schwartz

FLIGHT ATTENDANT
Don't worry.
You'll be home soon.

TED
I'm not going home.

FLIGHT ATTENDANT
Don't worry.
You'll be home sooner or later.

TED
I'm never going home.
Am I dead?

FLIGHT ATTENDANT
Stunned.
Is there anything you want?
Pillow?
Blanket?
Headset?

TED
What happens now?

FLIGHT ATTENDANT
Soda?
Diet soda?
V8?

TED
What happens now?

FLIGHT ATTENDANT
Peanuts?

TED
What happens now?

FLIGHT ATTENDANT
Pretzels?

TED
What happens now?

FLIGHT ATTENDANT
There's no need to panic, but you certainly shouldn't relax.

LANIE
Why?

MEL
Bundle up.

LANIE
Why?

MEL
You'll get frostbite.

LANIE
Why?

MEL
Because I said.

LANIE
Why?

MEL
Ask your father.
Call him up and ask him.

LANIE
I bet he's on the plane.

MEL
I bet he's on the prowl.

FLIGHT ATTENDANT
Sorry.
I don't make the rules.

TED
Isn't it a rule that you can never go home again?

FLIGHT ATTENDANT
Don't worry.
You'll be home soon.

TED
Isn't it a rule that home is where the heart is?

FLIGHT ATTENDANT
Don't worry.
You'll be home sooner or later.

TED
Isn't it a rule that everything we want we already have?

FLIGHT ATTENDANT
Is there anything you want?

TED
I want to watch my son grow up and get married.
Or grow up and not get married.
I don't care if my son gets married.
I just want my son to grow up and be happy.
I just want my son to grow old and be safe.
I just want my son to outlive me by a million and one years.
By a million and two years.
I just want my son to outlive me by a million and three years.
I just want my tears to roll up my face instead of down my
    face.

I just want my tears to defy the laws of gravity.
I just want my son to defy the laws of nature.
I just want a drink.

FLIGHT ATTENDANT
Alcoholic beverages are four dollars.

TED
I just want another drink.

FLIGHT ATTENDANT
Alcoholic beverages are three euros.

TED
One night, I don't know when, last year sometime, I got home
    from work, and I was tired, and I changed out of my
    clothes, and I went in to watch TV.
A few minutes later, my son came in, and he had this
    enormous grin on his face.
He had snuck into my room and put on the clothes that I had
    just taken off.
My jacket, my tie, my shoes, everything.
And he was so proud.
And I was so tired.
And I screamed at him.
At the top of my lungs.
I screamed at him.
"LOOK AT YOU!
YOU'RE RUINING EVERYTHING!"
Why?

FLIGHT ATTENDANT
I don't know.

TED
What for?

FLIGHT ATTENDANT
I can't say.

TED
And he cried.

FLIGHT ATTENDANT
Of course.

TED
And he went away.

FLIGHT ATTENDANT
Of course.

TED
I just want to take it back.

FLIGHT ATTENDANT
Alcoholic beverages are forty-four pesos.

TED
I just want to buy my son every action figure in the history of
    action figures.

FLIGHT ATTENDANT
Alcoholic beverages are four hundred rubles.

TED
He wouldn't have to share them.
I just want to watch my son outgrow his action figures.

FLIGHT ATTENDANT
Had I the lips, the tongue, the mouth, the song of Orpheus, I'd
    go beneath the earth and bring him back, and sing him
    back, I'd sing him back.

TED
I just want to bring him back.

FLIGHT ATTENDANT
Alcoholic beverages are one hundred yen.

TED
I have a question.

FLIGHT ATTENDANT
I have an answer.

LANIE
Are snowmen always men?

TED
Am I dead?

FLIGHT ATTENDANT
Stunned.

TED
I have a question.

FLIGHT ATTENDANT
I have an answer.

MEL
Are call girls always girls?

TED
Am I dead?

FLIGHT ATTENDANT
Stunned.

TED
I have a question.

FLIGHT ATTENDANT
I have an answer.

LANIE
What's a call girl?

MEL
Ask your father.
Call him up and ask him.

TED
Am I dead?

FLIGHT ATTENDANT
What part of *stunned* don't you understand?

LANIE
I bet he's asleep.

MEL
I bet he's with a call girl.

TED
I wish I were dead.

LANIE
I wish I were Helen Keller.

FLIGHT ATTENDANT
How do you feel?

TED
Like a recent college grad.
I feel like I need a new wardrobe.

FLIGHT ATTENDANT
There's no need to panic, but you certainly shouldn't relax.

MEL
Ow.

LANIE
What's frostbite?
Does it have to do with teeth?

MEL
Ow.

LANIE
Is my guess as good as yours?

MEL
Ow.
I stepped on an action figure.
I stepped on another.
They're everywhere.
Underfoot.
I'm going to take them outside and bury them.

LANIE
Can I help?

MEL
Help me.

LANIE
Can I help?

MEL
Help me help myself.

Interlude: Guy and Lenora sing a song.

An airport lounge.

GUY AND LENORA
> *Here in the underworld.*
> *Here in the underworld.*
> *Here in the underworld.*
> *I'm sitting.*

GUY	**LENORA**
And watching.	*I'm waiting.*
UNC lose to	*For Bombay Sapphire*
Tennessee	*Or Ketel One*
And Texas A&M	*Or Belvedere*
Up by nine	*Or Tanqueray*
And Pebble Beach	*Or Belvedere*
And Notre Dame	*Or Tanqueray*
And even tennis	*Or even Gordon's*
And even bowling	*Or even Smirnoff*
And waiting.	*And waiting.*

GUY AND LENORA
> *It was never my intention to give so much attention*

LENORA
> *To drinks*

GUY
> *To sports*
> *To golf links*

LENORA
> *To airports*

GUY
> *To tomato juice*

LENORA

To married men
To Grey Goose

GUY AND LENORA

To CNN.
Here in the underworld.
It makes me feel
It makes me feel as if
It makes me feel as if
I could call someone back from the dead.

Scene 4

A bar. TED *is drinking beer and watching the game. So is some guy named* GUY.

GUY
Is your wife a wife-wife?
Or is she one of those take-charge, split-your-lip, bust-your-
    balls, pull-your-chain, cook-your-goose, get-your-goat, rip-
    you-to-shreds, kick-you-when-you're-down types of gals?

TED
Somethin' like that.

GUY
Best a both, huh?
Lucky guy.
Lucky guy.
Lucky guy.

TED
You want her?
Take her.
She's yours.

GUY
Free of charge?

TED
Small fee.

GUY
Thanks.
Thanks, man.

Generous offer.
You got a generous spirit.
And that's a rare thing to come by in this day and age.
Trust me on that.
Take it from me.
Trust me on that.
Take it from me.
But I got my own little lady back home to contend with, if you
    know what I mean.
You know what I mean.
How much we talkin'?

TED
Zero down.

GUY
Money-back guarantee?

TED
No questions asked.

GUY
You got a recent photo or what?

TED *hands* GUY *a photo.*

TED
Her name's Mel.
Short for Melanoma.
But you can change it.

GUY
Say, not bad.
Those your kids?

TED
Those?
No.

No.

Those are . . .

No.

I should warn you, though, because you can't really tell in the
    picture:

Her vagina is green and her urine is blue.

GUY

Green, huh?

What, you mean, like, fertile ground?

Or, like, green with envy?

Or, like, cold . . . hard . . . cash?

TED

Somethin' like that.

GUY

And is it a green-green or, like, more like a pastel?

TED

Actually, it's—

Well, I don't want to say lime, but—

GUY

And is this a permanent situation or—

TED

Let me put it this way:

If she's wearing, say, a green camisole or a green bustier or a
    green negligé or what have you, it might bring out the
    green in her vagina.

Or it might not.

Vaginas are . . .

What's the word?

GUY

Mercurial.

TED
Mercurial.
But it's really only a slight hue.
I just thought I should mention it because of . . .

GUY
Company policy.

TED
Company policy.
So what do you think?
Take her out for a test drive?
Little spin around the block?
One-time offer.
Won't last.
Vaginas sell themselves.

GUY
Does she need a lot of light?

TED
A little.

GUY
Water?

TED
The usual.

GUY
Wish I could.
Wish I could.
Wish I could.
But like I said, I got my own little lady back home to contend
    with, if you know what I mean.
You know what I mean.
How 'bout we do a trade?
My little lady for your little lady?

TED
For keeps?

GUY
Trial basis.
And if we're not completely satisfied, then no big deal, no
    harm done, no big whoop, no sweat.
I think I got a recent photo here someplace.

GUY *hands* TED *a photo.*

Her name's Meg.
Short for Smegma.
But you can change it.

TED *(looking at the photo)*
That your daughter?

GUY
Sure is.

TED
That your son?

GUY
Sure was.

TED
Huh . . .
I thought you said your little lady was a little lady.

GUY
Did I?
No kidding.

TED
Don't kid a kidder.

GUY
Did I?
No shit.

TED
Don't shit a shitter.

GUY
Now, don't get me wrong.
I love her to death and all.
She's the mother of my kid and crap.
But between you, me, and the lamppost, my little lady is not
    the little lady I married.
How 'bout Melanoma?

TED
Can I have my recent photo back?

GUY
Is she the little lady *you* married?

TED
Gimme my recent photo back.

GUY
Gimme gimme never gets.
Crybaby.

TED
Who you calling crybaby?

GUY
Wuss.

TED
Who you calling wimp?

GUY
Creep.

TED
Who you calling loser?

GUY
Moron.

TED
Who you calling reject?

GUY
Lamebrain.

TED
Who you calling jerk off?

GUY
Jackass.

TED
Who you calling candy ass?

GUY
Limp dick.

TED
Who you calling pecker head?

GUY
Pansy.

TED
GIMME MY FREAKIN' PHOTO!

GUY
TAKE YOUR FREAKIN' PHOTO!

TED
YOUR WIFE DOESN'T KNOW DICK ABOUT DICK!

GUY *gives* TED *back his photo. They calm down.*

What's your favorite part of your job?

GUY
I'm a people person.

TED
I like numbers.

GUY
It's not that I *don't* like numbers . . .

TED *(telling a joke)*
What's the difference between your wife and your job?

GUY
What?

TED
After twenty years, your job still sucks.

GUY
Beauty is in the eye of the beer holder.

TED
Good one.

GUY
Beauty is in the eye of the beer holder.

TED
Good one.

GUY
Beauty is in the eye of the beer holder.

TED
Good one.

They laugh.

GUY *(seriously)*
I feel for you.
Is all I'm sayin'.
I feel for you.

TED
I don't know you from a hole in the wall.

GUY
I don't know you from Adam.

TED
I don't know you from Adam's house cat.

GUY
Beat it.

TED
Can it.

GUY
Shove it.

TED
Save it.

GUY *(giving him the finger)*
Save this!
I don't know you from a hole in the ground.

But I feel for you.
Man.

TED
Hey, man, don't call me "man."

GUY
Sorry, man.

TED (*giving him the finger*)
Feel this!

Scene 5

MEL *and* LANIE *are burying action figures in the snow.*

MEL
A call girl is a girl that you call.

LANIE
Why?

MEL
Because you're lonely.

LANIE
Why?

MEL
Because you're bored.

LANIE
Why?

MEL
Because you're weak.

LANIE
Why?

MEL
Because you're pathetic.

LANIE
I want a call girl for Christmas.

MEL
Christmas is over.

LANIE
I want a call girl for next Christmas.

MEL
Christmas is never coming back.

LANIE
I want a call girl now.

MEL
You can't have one now.

LANIE
Why?

MEL
Because call girls are for grown men.

LANIE
Why?

MEL
Because you're a little girl.

LANIE
Why?

MEL
Because that's the way God made you.

LANIE
Why?

MEL
Because God has a master plan.

Jenny Schwartz

LANIE
He does?

MEL
Maybe.

LANIE
He does?

MEL
Maybe not.

LANIE
I want a master plan for my birthday.

MEL
Your birthday is over.

LANIE
I want a master plan for my next birthday.

MEL
Your birthday is never coming back.

LANIE
I want a master plan now.

MEL
You can't have one now.

LANIE
Why?

MEL
Because master plans are overrated.

LANIE
Why?

MEL
Because master plans are overpriced.

LANIE
Why?

MEL
Because master plans are underfunded.

LANIE
Why?

MEL
Because master plans are all sold out.

LANIE
I want to be a grown man.

MEL
Don't be silly.
You want to be Helen Keller.

LANIE
I want God to make me into a grown man.

MEL
Don't be silly.
You want God to make you into Helen Keller.

LANIE
Grown men are the luckiest.

MEL
Helen Keller was lucky.

LANIE
Helen Keller wasn't lucky.

MEL
Helen Keller was very lucky.

LANIE
Why?

MEL
Because Helen Keller endured the unendurable.

LANIE
Why?

MEL
Because Helen Keller achieved the unachievable.

LANIE
Why?

MEL
Because Helen Keller surpassed the unsurpassable.

LANIE
Why?

MEL
Because Helen Keller stood the test of time.

LANIE
I want to stand the test of time.

MEL
Don't be silly.
You have to be dead to stand the test of time.

LANIE
Oh.

MEL
You have to be a dead grown man to stand the test of time.

LANIE
Oh.
Helen Keller wasn't a dead grown man.

MEL
Helen Keller was an exception to the rule.

LANIE
I want to be an exception to the rule for Halloween.

MEL
Halloween is over.

LANIE
I want to be an exception to the rule for next Halloween.

MEL
Halloween is never coming back.

LANIE
I want to be an exception to the rule now.

MEL
You can't be one now.

LANIE
Why?

MEL
Because you have to be foreign to be an exception to the rule.

LANIE
Why?

MEL
Because you have to be weird to be an exception to the rule.

LANIE
Why?

MEL
Because you have to be eight to be an exception to the rule.

LANIE
Why?

MEL
Because "*i* before *e* except after *c*."

LANIE
I want to be eight.

MEL
You will.
If you're lucky.

LANIE
I want to be lucky.

MEL
You will.
If you're weird.

LANIE
I want to be weird.

MEL
You will.
If you're foreign.

LANIE
I don't get it.

MEL
Don't be silly.
There's nothing to get.

LANIE
I want to be a dead grown man.

MEL
I'll see what I can do.

LANIE
I want to be a dead grown man who stood the test of time.

MEL
I'll see what I can do.

LANIE
I want to be a dead grown man who stood the test of time
with a master plan.

MEL
I'll see what I can do.

THE TOOTH FAIRY *reappears.*

THE TOOTH FAIRY
The apple doesn't fall far from the tree.

MEL
The tooth fairy says the apple doesn't fall far from the tree.

LANIE
Did you know that razor blades hide in apples, and when you
bite into them, they slice up your mouth and cut up your
throat, and you can't scream for help because your tongue
is missing and your vocal cords are gone?

MEL
The tooth fairy says you're going to follow in my footsteps.

LANIE
But what if I hate you?
But what if I hate your fat footsteps?

THE TOOTH FAIRY
Hate is a form of love.

MEL
Good news.
Hate is a form of love.

LANIE
Not in my book.

MEL
You don't have a book.

LANIE
Not in my book, it isn't.

MEL
You're too young to have a book.

On the night you were born, it was snowing and raining at the
    exact same time.
And it looked like the lake was boiling.

LANIE
Boiling . . .

MEL
And the fog was thick.
Like soup.
And it took forever to get to the hospital.
And then, I pushed and pushed, but you were stuck.

And then, you were in distress.
And then, it was the longest minute of my life.
Except for this one.

LANIE
And then what?

MEL
The end.

LANIE
Hey, you skipped my favorite part where I was a girl.

MEL
Don't play favorites.

LANIE
Takes one to know one.

MEL
I know you are, but what am I?

LANIE
Let that be a lesson to you.

MEL
You started it.

LANIE
Serves you right.
Let's play house.

MEL
Don't be silly.
There's no one to play with.

LANIE
Let's play hide-and-seek.

MEL
Don't be silly.
There's no place to hide.

LANIE
Let's play tag.

THE TOOTH FAIRY
You can run, but you just can't hide.

MEL
Bad news.
You can run, but you just can't hide.

Interlude: Guy sings a song.

GUY
These are a few things you cannot sell on eBay:
Alcohol.
Pets.
Babies.
Drugs.
Even prescription drugs.
Credit cards.
Encouragement of illegal activity.
Firearms and knives.
Chemicals and combustibles.
Intellectual property.
Livestock.
Lottery tickets.
Stolen stuff.
Human body parts or remains.
Used cosmetics.
These are a few things you cannot sell on eBay.

Scene 6

A lounge. TED *and some lady named* LENORA *are at a table with drinks.*

TED
My daughter's six and my son is dead.
Ted.
Ten.
You'll have to forgive me.
I'm not usually this—

LENORA
I am!

TED
—drunk.

LENORA
Ask anyone!

TED
Let me start over.

LENORA
You should see my liver, later, liver, later, liver, later.

TED
I'm Ted and my son is—

LENORA
Pleased to meet you!

Jenny Schwartz

TED

—ten.

LENORA

Likewise I'm sure!
Help me with your name.

TED

We almost lost him, though.
One summer.
He swallowed a box of—

LENORA

Ow!

TED

Pushpins.

LENORA

Wow!

TED

You're tellin' me.
But we pumped his stomach, so . . .

LENORA

Where I come from, they're called thumbtacks, pushpins,
     thumbtacks, pushpins.

TED

I'm kidding.

LENORA

I'm not.

TED

He swallowed a box of Wheat Thins.

LENORA
You must be very proud.

TED
We am.
I.
Were.
We was.

LENORA
Pushpins, Wheat Thins, thumbtacks, Cracker Jacks.
You're dead and your son's Fred and he swallowed a box of—

TED
Correct!

LENORA
But you punched his stomach, so—

TED
Correct!

LENORA
May both of you rest in—

TED
Death is a fact of—

LENORA
Life is short!

TED
Life is a shrimp!

LENORA
Life is a shrimp and then you die!

Jenny Schwartz

TED
I'll drink to that!

LENORA
Hear hear!

They kiss.

Mmm.
Martini.
Where were we?
Shrimp.
Sucks to be a shrimp.
Crustaceans have no bones.

TED
I like your bones.

LENORA
All of them?

TED
I like your bone structure.
I want to suck on your bones.

LENORA
All of them?

TED
I want to suck on your bone structure.

LENORA
Do you have a problem with condoms?
Just so you know, I'm disease free, and I fully intend to—
    (handing him a note)
See.

TED
What's this?

LENORA
A note from my doctor.
It's laminated.
Are *you*?

TED
Disease free?

LENORA
Laminated?

TED
I think so.

LENORA
I thought so.

TED
The last time I—

LENORA *(bringing her fingers to his throat)*
Let me check—

TED
I like it when you check my pulse.

LENORA
I like it too.

TED
I like it when you like it too.
It's better that way.

LENORA
You can tell a lot about a man by his pulse.

My ex, for instance, you can tell by his pulse, that (a) he's
    dehydrated, and (b) he's sick and twisted, and (c) he doesn't
    want to be tied down.
And I'm like, "No problem. Neither do I."
And so I buy him a watch.
Gold plated.
And I get it engraved.
Genuine leather.
And he's like, "Is it waterproof?"
And I'm like, "It's engraved."
And he's like, "Is it waterproof?"
And I'm like, "It's engraved."
And he's like, "Is it waterproof?"
And I'm like, "It's engraved."
And he's like, "A figure eight?"
And I'm like, "An infinity sign."
And he's like, "A figure eight?"
And I'm like, "An infinity sign."
And he's like, "A figure eight?"
And I'm like, "An infinity sign."
And he's like, "Because time is infinite?"
And I'm like, "Because love is infinite."
And he's like, "I told you from the start . . ."
And I'm like, "Who is that in the background?"
And he's like, "Francine."
And I'm like, "My cousin?"
And he's like, "She's hot."
And I'm like, "I'm pregnant."
And he's like, "Get rid of it."
And I'm like, "I'm thirty-five."
And he's like, "You're thirty-nine."
And I'm like, "I'm thirty-five."
And he's like, "You're thirty-nine."
And I'm like, "I'm thirty-five."
And he's like, "You're a train wreck."
And I'm like, "I need you in my life."
And he's like, "You're damaged goods."
And I'm like, "I need you in my life."

And he's like, "You wanna have a three-way?"
And I'm like, "Isn't that incest?"
And he's like, "Forget it."
And so I go over.
And I ring the bell.
And I know they're in there.
And I bang on the door.
And I guess I pass out.
And the next thing I know, there's a foot in my face.
And I'm like, "Where are you going?"
And they're like, "Starbucks."
And I'm like, "Wait up."
And they're like, "Go home."
And I'm like, "Francine, how can you do this to me, Francine?"
And he's like, "Francine can't help it if she's hot. Can you,
    Francine?"
And she's like, "No, not really, no."
And I'm like, "Haven't you ever heard of loyalty?"
And they're like, "Haven't you ever heard of fetal alcohol
    syndrome?"
And I'm like, "I'm not even going to dignify that with a
    response."

TED
Am I dehydrated?

LENORA *(feeding him an ice cube)*
Have an ice cube.

TED
Am I sick and twisted?

LENORA
You're fair and square.
Are you a politician?
You look like a politician.
Didn't I see you on C-SPAN?

TED

I like it when you feed me.

LENORA

I like it when you chew me up and spit me out and spit me up
    and chew me out and hang me out to dry.

TED

I like it when you need me in your life.

LENORA

I need you in my life like I need another foot in my face.

TED

I like it when you need another foot in your face.

LENORA

I do need another foot in my face.
Bad.
I need it bad.
And while you're at it, stick another fork in my eye.

TED

I like it when you need it bad.

LENORA

I'll take what I can get, if you know what I mean.

TED

I know what you mean.

LENORA

I know what I mean too.

TED

I like it when you know what I mean too.

LENORA

And then he takes off the watch and throws it at me and I'm
   thinking, you know what I'm thinking, "Catch it or move
   or blink, Lenora. Catch it or move or blink."

TED

And then what happens?

LENORA

Three guesses.

TED

You blink?

LENORA

I barf.

TED

I like it when I look like a politician.

LENORA

Hey, wait a minute here, you're not gonna get all kinky on me,
   are you?
Because contrary to popular, because contrary to popular,
   because contrary to popular, because contrary to popular,
I'm not that kind of a—
Who am I kidding?
Kinky's my middle name.
You name it, I invented it.
Basically.
Do you have a middle name, Fred?

TED

Ted.

LENORA

Did we just have our first fight, Fred?

TED
Ted.

LENORA
Tell me, Fred-Ted, do you know any tricks?

TED
I don't think so.

LENORA
Jokes?

TED
I don't know.
I can whistle.

LENORA
Can you wrestle?

TED
I can parallel park.

LENORA
Well, aren't you a regular Houdini.

They kiss.

Whodunit.

They kiss.

Houdini.

They kiss.

TED
Why was Helen Keller's leg yellow?

LENORA
Why?

TED
Because her dog was blind too.

LENORA
Huh?

TED
Because her dog was blind too.

LENORA
Huh?

TED
Because her dog—

LENORA
Oh!
Oh!
Because her dog . . .
So he peed . . .
So her leg . . .
That's crazy!
That's insane!
That's the craziest thing I ever heard!
Oh my God!
Will you look at me!
I'm crying!
I'm totally crying!
Look at me!
Will you look at me?
Oh my God!
I'm totally dying!
He was blind!
Helen Keller!
Oh my God!

Jenny Schwartz

Her dog was blind!
I love you, Fred-Ted!
I love everything about you!
Were your parents poets?

TED
I should tell you—

LENORA
I appreciate your honesty.

TED
I'm a married man.

LENORA
Aren't we all?
In some ways?
Poets?
My point being that as an independent woman of what used to
   be the nineties, I love you from the bottom of what used
   to be my heart.

TED
Thanks.

LENORA
Sure.

TED
You mean it?

LENORA
Would I lie?

TED
It's been so long since I've been on the receiving end of a
   compliment.

They kiss.

LENORA
Did she really have a dog?
Helen Keller?

TED
She may have had.

LENORA
But was he blind?
Pets are therapeutic.
So they say.
I wouldn't know.
I'm allergic.
To everything.
To anything organic.
I'm having an allergic reaction right now.
Are you organic?

TED
I think so.

LENORA
I thought so.

They kiss.

Mmm.
Martini.
Where were we?
Houdini.
I love olives.
I love pimentos.
I love cocktail onions.
I love cocktail napkins.
I love lemon wedges.

I love lime wedges.
I love mini–paper umbrellas.
I love mini–plastic swords.
I just have so much love and nowhere to put it.

TED
I'll take it.

LENORA
You want it?

TED
Gladly.

LENORA
Great.

They kiss.

TED
Why can't Helen Keller drive?

They kiss.

LENORA
Why?

They kiss.

TED
Because she's a woman.

They kiss.

Why can't Helen Keller drive?

They kiss.

LENORA
Why?

They kiss.

TED
Because she's dead.

LENORA
I have a mute half sister.
Last I heard, she lived in Tucson.
I haven't ever met her, but I know she's out there.
Staring.
You been to Tucson?

TED
We flew to Sante Fe.
And then we drove to Albuquerque.
And then to the Four Corners.
And then to the Grand Canyon.
And then we drove to Phoenix.
And then we flew home.
My kids, the whole time, they were fighting over the armrest.
They liked the Four Corners, though.
Hopping back and forth.
We skipped Tucson.

LENORA
I don't blame you.

TED
Can you blame us?

LENORA
I'd be scared too.
That the car would drive off and leave me with my sister.
The mutant.

TED

There's a town in Utah called American Fork.
We didn't make it up there, but we saw it on the map.
We circled it.

LENORA

Someday I'm gonna find her.
Bring her a cat.
Call it Puss.
After Oedipus.
From the Bible.
She'd like that, I think.
Get a kick out of it, I think.
Pets are therapeutic.
So they say.
I wouldn't know.
I'm allergic.
To everything.
To anything organic.
I'm having an allergic reaction right now.
Are you organic?

TED

I think so.

LENORA

I thought so.

They kiss.

TED

I've never done this before.
Lately, I have.
Thought about it.
Looked around.
Sometimes, I take off my ring.
In my head, I'm a widower.

LENORA
Why not a bachelor?

TED
I have to account for the loss on my face.

LENORA
You do have loss on your face.
I was pretending not to notice.
Do I?

TED
Maybe a little.
In your teeth.

LENORA
Where?

TED
Up here.

LENORA
Hang on.

TED
By all means.

LENORA
Are you sure it's not spinach?

TED
Spinach is green.

LENORA
I used to be a drunk.
Ask anyone.
You should have seen my liver.

Jenny Schwartz

But now, I wake up in the morning, and I take a look around,
    and I see the world exactly as it is.
No better.
No worse.
And I take pride in everything I do.
My friends are like, "What's up with *you*?"
And I'm like, "I've found love in the twenty-first century.
It's about space and choice and a terrific sense of freedom."
And they're like, "Who is this guy?
Does he have a brother or what?"
And I'm like, "He's a politician.
You've probably seen him on C-SPAN.
It's great because he's out all day . . . saving schools . . . waging
    wars . . .
And at night, he comes home, and he cries on my shoulder,
    and I tell him, everything's gonna be okay."
And he's like, "How do you know?"
And I'm like, "I just know."
And he's like, "How do you know?"
And I'm like, "I just know."
And he's like, "How do you know?"
And I'm like, "Trust me."
And he's like, "I trust you."
And I'm like, "Trust is my favorite foundation."
And he's like, "Loyalty, thy name is Lenora."

TED
Let's go.
Right now.
You and me.
Against the world.
We'll drive cross country.
I'll parallel park.

LENORA
Naked?

TED
Absolutely.

LENORA
With the top down?

TED
Why not?

LENORA
To American Fork!

TED
To American Fork!

LENORA
To American Fork-in-the-eye!

TED
To American Fork-in-the-eye!

They kiss.

LENORA
"In the land of the blind, the one-eyed man is king!"

TED
Huh? . . .
"He who's most dangerous sleeps with his eyes open!"

LENORA
Huh? . . .

TED
Where are you from, anyway?

LENORA
Originally?
All over.
You?

TED
Me too.

LENORA
Do you think we know any of the same people?

TED
We both know our waitress.

LENORA
That's true.
We both know Sharon.

TED
But Sharon doesn't know us.

LENORA
No.

TED
So Sharon doesn't count.
Are you involved?

LENORA
With a man?
Maybe.

TED
With a woman?

LENORA
Why do you ask?
Do I have lesbian in my eye?

TED
I thought so for a second.
But now I can see it's just . . .
Sex.

LENORA
I don't like you.
But I like your type.
Do you have any friends you could set me up with?

TED *(looking at her birthmark)*
I have a friend who has the exact same birthmark.
Where did you say you were born?

LENORA
Do you live around here?
Or work around here?
Or both?

TED
Neither.

LENORA
Likewise.
I'm rarely in this part of town.

They kiss.

Tell me something, stranger to stranger: Am I a train wreck?

They kiss.

Tell me something, stranger to stranger: Am I damaged goods?

They kiss.

Interlude: The Flight Attendant sings a song.

FLIGHT ATTENDANT
Ladies and Gentlemen,
The captain has turned on the fasten-seat-belt sign.
Please remain in your seats.

In case of emergency,
Please remain calm.

If the oxygen masks descend,
Place your mask over your face,
Before placing your child's mask over his or her face.
Please remain calm.

If the plane should suddenly descend.
Or the wings should fall off.
Please remain calm.

If fire should engulf the cabin.
Or other passengers are raptured.
Or we land in choppy waters.
Please remain calm.

If you are uncomfortable sitting in an exit row,
Please contact your flight attendant.
Please remain calm.
Please remain calm.

TED
Ma'am?

FLIGHT ATTENDANT
You rang?

TED
I'm uncomfortable sitting in an exit row.

FLIGHT ATTENDANT
Right this way.
Sir.

TED *follows* FLIGHT ATTENDANT *away.*

LANIE
Dad!

TED
Lanie!

LANIE
Is there a McDonald's around here?

TED
If I believe in God, and I do believe in God, I'd have to say
    there's a McDonald's around here someplace.
One McTickle coming right up . . .

MEL *(to* TED, *as if on the phone)*
What are you doing?

TED *(as if on the phone, watching TV)*
Nothing.
I don't know.
What's it called.

MEL
Me too.

TED
With the cop and the cop and the lawyer and the judge.
It's an old one.
About a suitcase.
And a kid inside.
And they find him, but . . .
No dice.
Huh . . .

MEL
Who's winning?

TED
Hard to say.

MEL
Take a stab.

TED
The other guys.

LANIE *(to* MEL*)*
Tell me all about childbirth.

MEL
Well, first of all, there are lots of things that no one tells you.
And then, you give birth to the placenta.

LANIE
Does it hurt?
Childbirth?

MEL
You can't remember pain.

LANIE
I remember when I pencil-sharpened my pinky.

MEL
I suppose I remember my paper cut.
Ow.

When I was pregnant with Sam, the dog got sick.
I went to give her a pill, and I don't know what came over me,
     but I took it myself.
I just popped it in my mouth and swallowed it down.
A big, green pill with a big glass of water.

I was seven months pregnant.

I wasn't thinking.

I don't know what I was thinking.

After about ten minutes, I realized what I had done.

God, I was worried.

I was so worried.

My baby . . .

What have I done to my baby?

I tried to throw it up, but it wouldn't come out.

It was somewhere inside me.

Dissolving.

But then, Sam was fine, and I was fine, and the dog was fine, and three years later, you were born, and you were fine too, and for a fraction of a second, we were, all of us together, fine, just fine, no . . . happy.

Terribly.

Oh . . .

Oh God . . .

Why was I always worried about the wrong things?

LANIE
What's a fraction?

MEL
A fraction is a piece of pie.
A call girl is a piece of ass.

THE TOOTH FAIRY *reappears.*

THE TOOTH FAIRY
Happiness is fleeting.

MEL
The tooth fairy says happiness is fleeting.

GI JOE *appears.*

GI JOE
GI Joe says, "Knowing is half the battle."

MEL
But we buried you.

GI JOE
I escaped.

MEL
Didn't we bury you?

GI JOE
I escaped.

MEL *(introducing them)*
GI Joe, the tooth fairy.
The tooth fairy, GI Joe.

GI JOE
We've met.

THE TOOTH FAIRY
We have a history.

GI JOE
We have a history.

THE TOOTH FAIRY
We've met.

TED *(to* MEL, *as if answering the phone)*
Hi.

MEL *(to* TED, *as if on the phone)*
It's me.

TED
I know.

MEL
Hi.

TED
What are you doing?

MEL
Living and learning.

TED
Anything going on?

MEL
We have new neighbors.
As of last week.
As of the week before.
They're quiet as mice, but I know what they're up to.
Eating.
Sleeping.
Having sex.
We have new neighbors.
As of the week before, the week before, the week before.
I haven't yet met them, but I'm planning on it.
When the time is right.
Pop on over in my Sunday best.
Smile and say, "Can I pretty please borrow some legs?"

TED
Eggs?

MEL *(to* THE TOOTH FAIRY*)*
My son, his teeth, I need them.
Do you have them?
I'd like to make a necklace.

I used to be crafty.
In the best sense of the word.

THE TOOTH FAIRY
I don't keep the teeth.
I give them back.

MEL
Back?

THE TOOTH FAIRY
Back to God.

MEL
Why to God?
What does he want with them?

THE TOOTH FAIRY
Well, for starters, he's not a *he*, now is he, now?

MEL
The tooth fairy hates me.

THE TOOTH FAIRY
You shouldn't say "hates."
It's a five-letter word.

GI JOE *(to* MEL*)*
You know what they say about God?

MEL
What?

GI JOE
He helps those who help themselves.
You're in the driver's seat.
It's your finger on the trigger.

Mind over matter.
What's the matter?
Your mind.
To be all that you can be.
Or not to be all that you can be.
That is the question.
Now, drop and give me twenty.

MEL
But we buried you.

GI JOE
I escaped.

MEL
Didn't we bury you?

GI JOE
I escaped.

TED
Hi.

MEL
It's me.

TED
I know.

MEL
Hi.

TED
What are you doing?

MEL
Sitting and spinning.

TED
Anything going on?

MEL
I got my period.
This morning.
In the mail.
In a big pink box.
With a big pink bow.
It looks so pretty.
The packaging.
I hate to open it.
So I'm sending it back.
Unless you want it.

TED
Thanks.

MEL
No backsies.

TED
My day was long and grueling too.
Not that you asked.

MEL
How was your day?

TED
Same old same old.
Mind your own business.
Cut the crap.
Do you know how little affection I feel from you?
From you, I said.
Not *for* you.
From you, I said.
Not *for* you.
What are you doing?

MEL
Cutting the crap.

TED
Say something nice.

MEL
Something nice.

TED
What's up?

MEL (*to* THE TOOTH FAIRY *and* GI JOE)
I'd like to run away.
Disappear.
Change my name.

THE TOOTH FAIRY
What's the use?
You'd still have lower-back pain.

GI JOE
You'd still be frightened of the chiropractor.

THE TOOTH FAIRY
It's the way she was raised.

GI JOE
Her parents, they were frightened of everything.
Of anything tactile.

THE TOOTH FAIRY
Tangible.

GI JOE
Corporeal.

THE TOOTH FAIRY
Material.

GI JOE
Maternal?

THE TOOTH FAIRY
I think so.

GI JOE
I thought so.

GI JOE *disappears.*

MEL *(to* TED*)*
What are you doing?
Let me guess.
Nothing.
What are you watching?
Let me guess.
Porn.
I'm not a prude.
I'm hardly a prude.
I watch porn.
Myself.
On occasion.
To digest.
After lunch.
With the vacuum cleaner.
No, I mean, no, I mean—not what you're thinking.
You're disgusting.
Your mind.
Where it goes.
It's disgusting.
You should be ashamed.
I hope you're ashamed.
You should be put away.
I hope you're put away.

Jenny Schwartz

IF YOU WANT TO WATCH PORN, WATCH PORN!
Let's have phone sex.

TED
I'm exhausted.
My head is pounding.

MEL
I'm exhilarated.
My vagina is glowing.
Like kryptonite.
Like a phosphorescent lake.

TED
You have no idea what I do all day.

MEL
You have no idea what I'm wearing.
I bought a new—
What's it called?
Nightie.
Silk.
Sea-foam green.
It clings to my body like that stuff in the kitchen.
Saran Wrap.
Touch me.
Hold me.
Feel me.
Bitch-slap me.
Finger my phosphorescent lake.

TED
Are you peeing?

MEL
I'm chitchatting.
Excuse me while I pee.

LENORA *appears.*

LENORA *(to* TED*)*
You know what I could live on is finger food.
I like crudité.
I like canapé.
― You know what I could live on is nachos.
I like french fries.
I like cheese fries.
You know what I could live on is baby quiches.
You know what I could live on is baby lamb chops.
You know what I could live on is babies.
You just wanna eat 'em.
Don't you just wanna eat 'em?
You just wanna eat 'em.
Don't you just wanna eat 'em?

TED
Let's order.

LENORA
Should we order?

TED
Should we order?

LENORA
Let's order.

TED
I'm trying to decide between something and nothing.

LENORA
I'm trying to decide between nothing and something.
I'm not usually this heavy, but I recently had a baby.
Unfortunately—

TED
Did he die?

LENORA
He did.

TED
Anything I can do?

LENORA
Finger my phosphorescent lake.

TED
I just had a déjà vu.
And you were in it.

MEL *(to* TED*)*
Thanks, by the way, for my slippers.

TED
You like them?

MEL
I'm going to keep them.

LANIE *(referring to* TED *and* LENORA*)*
What are they doing?

MEL
He's sucking on her bone structure.

LANIE
Why?

MEL
It tastes good.

LANIE
What's bone structure?

MEL
I've heard it tastes good.

GUY *appears.*

GUY
Who are you rootin' for?

TED
Neither.
They both suck.

GUY
Suck this!

FLIGHT ATTENDANT *appears.*

FLIGHT ATTENDANT
I also like the call bell.
Situated above your head.
Go ahead.
Push it.
I'm more than happy to assist you.

TED
What's more than happy?

FLIGHT ATTENDANT
I'm more than happy to assist you.

TED
What's more than happy?

FLIGHT ATTENDANT
I'm more than happy to assist you.

LANIE
Does it hurt?
Childbirth?

MEL
You can't remember pain.

LANIE
I remember when I threw up a thumbtack.

MEL
I suppose I remember my funny bone.

LENORA, GUY, FLIGHT ATTENDANT, THE TOOTH FAIRY *(to* MEL*)*
Ha!

GUY
Why did God invent alcohol?

MEL
I give up.

GUY
So fat women could get laid too.

THE TOOTH FAIRY
What's funnier than a dead baby?

MEL
I give up.

THE TOOTH FAIRY
A dead baby in a clown costume.

FLIGHT ATTENDANT
What do you call a transvestite cow?

MEL
I give up.

FLIGHT ATTENDANT
A dairy queen.

LENORA
What was Helen Keller's favorite color?

MEL
I give up.

LENORA
Corduroy.

GUY
How can you tell if your wife is dead?

MEL
I give up.

GUY
The sex is the same, but the dishes pile up.

THE TOOTH FAIRY
Why did the baby cross the road?

MEL
I give up.

THE TOOTH FAIRY
It was stapled to the chicken.

FLIGHT ATTENDANT
What did the transvestite do for fun?

MEL
I give up.

FLIGHT ATTENDANT
Eat, drink, and be Mary.

LENORA
What did Helen Keller do when she fell down the well?

MEL
I give up.

LENORA
She screamed her hands off.

LANIE
Look, Ma!
No hands!

TED (to MEL)
Sit down.

MEL (to TED)
Tell me.

TED
Sit down.

MEL
Tell me.

GUY
Your wife's so fat, she used a mattress as a tampon.

TED
Your wife's so dumb, she tried to drown a fish.

GUY
Your wife's so fat, she has her own area code.

TED
Your wife's so nasty, she could make an onion cry.

LANIE
I'm crying.

LENORA, GUY, THE TOOTH FAIRY, FLIGHT ATTENDANT
Smile!
You're on *Candid Camera*!
Ha!

LANIE
Did you know that the tongue is a muscle?
Did you know that the dandelion is a weed?
Did you know that the sun is a star?
Did you know that the coconut is a seed?

Did you know that spiders are helpful?
Did you know that the earth is a magnet?
Did you know that tomatoes are fruit?
Did you know that whiskey is a spirit?

Did you know that hamsters eat their young?
Did you know that you can't lick your elbow?
Did you know that snails have sex with themselves?
Did you know that the bald eagle is a cymbal?

Did you know that one year for me is seven years for Snoopy?
Did you know that Snoopy is a beagle?
Did you know that Walt Disney is cryogenically frozen?
Did you know that suicide is illegal?

Did you know that avocados are the good kind of fat?
Did you know that our relatives are monkeys?
Did you know that we grow and grow until we're twenty-six,
    and then we start to atrophy?

Did you know that peanut butter and jelly are inextricably
    linked?
Did you know that Eskimos live in igloos?
Did you know that men are from Mars and women are from
    Venus?
Did you know that no news is good news?

Did you know that Peter Pan won't grow up?
Did you know that Jesus wept?
Did you know that George Washington cannot tell a lie?
Did you know that Latin died?

Did you know that Shakespeare was more than one person?
Did you know that bad things happen in threes?
Did you know that God is nondenominational?
Did you know that Grandma had two left feet?

Did you know that good things happen to bad people,
and bad things happen to good people,
and bad things happen to bad people,
and good things happen to good people?

Did you know that you can't get a sunburn through the
    window, but you can get cancer?

Did you know that kisses and hugs are better than drugs?

Did you know that you can pick your friends and you can pick
    your nose, but you just can't pick your friend's nose?

Did you know that our hearts are the same size as our fists?

But what if you have no hands?
What then?
But what if you have no hands?
What then?

God's Ear   131

TED
Hi.

MEL
It's me.

TED
I know.

MEL
Hi.

TED
What are you doing?

MEL
Reading and weeping.

TED
Anything going on?

MEL
I overwatered a plant.

TED
It happens.

MEL
No, it doesn't.

TED
These things happen.

MEL
No, they don't.

TED
I'm sorry.

MEL
I was going to say it's not your fault, but then I couldn't.

TED
What's up?

MEL
I should go.
Probably.
I should let you go.
Probably.
Bye.

TED
Why?

MEL
I said bye.

TED
I said why.

MEL
It's 10 p.m.
Do you know where your children are?

TED
Our children.

MEL
Our children.

TED
What do you want to do?

MEL
The tooth fairy suggests meditation.

THE TOOTH FAIRY
She coulda shoulda woulda made an excellent mother.

GI JOE
He coulda shoulda woulda made an excellent father.

LENORA *(to* GUY*)*
Have you ever meant nothing to someone?
Something to no one?

GUY *(to* LENORA*)*
I don't know.

LENORA
I don't know either.
I just have so much love and nowhere to put it.

GUY
I'll take it.

LENORA
You want it?

GUY
Gladly.

LENORA
Great.
I used to be secretly in love with you.

They kiss.

But now it's more out in the open.

They kiss.

GUY
Tell me something no one knows about you.

They kiss.

Except for maybe someone who forgot.

They kiss.

LENORA
Come home with me.
I'll show you my thread count.

GUY
I want to grab your ponytail.
And hang on for dear life.

LENORA
I want to finish your—

GUY
—sentences.

LENORA
Me—

GUY
—too.

GUY *and* LENORA *disappear.*

LANIE
What are they doing?

MEL
Where?

LANIE
Right there.

MEL
Oh, they're riding off into the horseshit.
Ha!

LANIE
You shouldn't say shit in front of the D-O-G.

MEL
The D-O-G hates me.

GI JOE *appears.*

GI JOE
How is the dog?

MEL
She has a lump in her throat.

GI JOE
How is the dog?

MEL
She wishes she had something to suck on.

GI JOE
How is the dog?

MEL
She's working on her upper-body strength every day, starting
    today.

GI JOE
How is the dog?

MEL
Easily, she bruises.

TED
Hi.

MEL
It's me.

TED
I know.

MEL
Hi.

TED
What are you doing?

MEL
Trying and failing.

TED
Anything going on?

MEL
There's a new sheriff in town.
And he's stalwart.
But I can't say I trust him.
I swear he keeps checking out my eggs.

TED
Legs?

GI JOE
How is the dog?

MEL
She's constantly on the verge of tears, but she just can't cry.

LANIE
I'm crying.

MEL
Bundle up!
You're on *Candid Camera*!

LANIE *(to* THE TOOTH FAIRY*)*
On the night I was born, it was snowing and raining at the
     exact same time.
And the fog was thick.
Like soup.
And it took forever to get to the hospital.
And then, she pushed and pushed, but I was stuck.
And then, I was in distress.
And then, it was the longest minute of her life.
Except for this one.
And then, the doctor said, "Here comes the baby, and it's a
     girl."
The end.
Oh and also, the lake was boiling.

MEL
Excuse me, but the lake wasn't boiling.

LANIE
Yes, it was.

MEL
No, it wasn't.

LANIE
The end.

MEL
The lake looked like it was boiling, but it wasn't really boiling.

LANIE
Yes, it was.

MEL
No, it wasn't.

LANIE
The end.

MEL
Lakes don't boil.
Not in real life.

LANIE
That's not what I heard.
The end.
I guess it was the weatherman who told my brother, and my
    brother told me, and now, I'm telling the tooth fairy.

MEL *(slapping* LANIE*)*
Liar!
There is no such thing as the tooth fairy.

LANIE *(slapping* MEL*)*
I heard it was boiling.
The end.

MEL
This morning, I woke up, and for a fraction of a second, I
    didn't know which one of you was dead.
And which one of you was alive.
And then, I remembered.
And then, I sat up.
And then, I looked life in the eye, and I winked.

LANIE
A fraction is a piece of pie.
A call girl is a piece of ass.

MEL *(to* THE TOOTH FAIRY*)*
My son, his teeth.
I want them back.

THE TOOTH FAIRY
No backsies.

MEL
I'd like to make a necklace.
I used to be crafty.

GI JOE
Crafty, my ass.
You're all thumbs.
Butterfingers.

MEL
But we buried you.

GI JOE
I escaped.

MEL
Didn't we bury you?

GI JOE
I escaped.

LANIE *(to* GI JOE*)*
Sir?

GI JOE
Present.

LANIE
Excuse me.
But I need to find my dad.

Jenny Schwartz

GI JOE
Hmmm . . .
Does he have a long face?

LANIE
I think I've got a recent photo here someplace.

She shows him a photo.

GI JOE
Right this way.
Miss.

GI JOE *leads* LANIE *away.*

MEL *and* TED *face each other. Slow. Lots of air.*

TED
Hold on.

MEL
Sure.

TED
Hold on a second.

MEL
Fine.

TED
Okay, I'm back.
I said I'm back.
Hello hello?

MEL
Sorry, wrong number.

TED
I'm back.

MEL
I said, "No backsies."

TED
Hello hello hello hello hello hello?
I'm back.

LANIE *finds* TED. *Slower. More air.*

LANIE
You look different.

TED
I do?

LANIE
Yes.
Did you grow?

TED
I don't think so.

LANIE
Did you shrink?

TED
Could be.

LANIE
That's silly.

TED
You're silly.

Jenny Schwartz

LANIE
What happened to your hair?

TED
Oh.
Right.
Well . . .
It turned gray.
A little.
Didn't it?

LANIE
Yes.
On the sides.

TED
I know.

LANIE
Why?

TED
Why?
Because of age . . .
I suppose . . .
And . . . genetics . . .
And also . . . probably because of . . .

LANIE
Sam?

TED
I was going to say *stress*.
Do you know how smart you are?
Do you know how very, very special?
Sometimes, I look at you, and I . . .

LANIE
Dad.

TED
Lanie.

LANIE
Can I see it?

TED
What?
You mean . . . ?

LANIE
Your hair.

TED *(kneeling down)*
Of course.

LANIE *(examining his hair)*
Oh.
Wow.
I like it.

TED
You do?

LANIE
Yes.

TED
Really?

LANIE
Yes.
A lot.

TED *(crying)*
Thank you.
I—
I can't even begin to tell you . . .

LANIE
Tell me what?
You're welcome.
What's wrong?
I like your beard.

TED
I have to shave.

LANIE
I lost a tooth.

They hold each other.

Shhh.
Oh.
You did shrink.

TED
You grew.

MEL *(to* THE TOOTH FAIRY *and* GI JOE*)*
When my son was in the lake, I was putting sunblock on my
    daughter.
Or at least I was trying.
She was stubborn and difficult.
You know how she gets.
"Enough already all right already enough already all right
    already."
But I wanted to be firm.
For once.
I wanted to stand my ground.
For once.

They asked us to consider organ donation.

They did.
They were gentle.

THE TOOTH FAIRY
And what did you tell them?

MEL
They were ever so gentle.

GI JOE
And what did you say?

MEL
I said,
"You have very fair skin, and it's my job to protect it."
I said,
"Hold still.
I'm just doing my job."
But she was crazed.
Hysterical.
Screaming her head off.
Thrashing around.
You would have thought I was trying to hurt her.
My child.
You would have thought I was causing her pain.
My child.
"You win,"
I said.
"I quit,"
I said.
"Go be someone else's daughter . . .
Get yourself another mother . . .
I don't want you anymore . . ."
And so she gave up.
Because she had no choice.
And she sat still.

Jenny Schwartz

Because she didn't have a choice.
I was meticulous.
Rapt.
I didn't miss a spot.
And when I finished.
When I finally, finally finished.
I stood up.
Pleased.
And I looked around,
Proud.
And he was . . .

TED *(to* MEL*)*
Sit down.

MEL *(to* TED*)*
Tell me.

TED
Sit down.

MEL
Tell me.

TED
He's gone.

THE TOOTH FAIRY *(to* MEL*, very simple and sweet)*
When your son was a baby, you would hold him in your arms
    for hours.
And you would just say hi.
"Hi hi hi hi."
For hours.
And then one day, when he was nine months old, he said it
    back.
Crystal clear.
You were sitting in the chair by the window.
And you couldn't believe your ears.

"Ted,"
you said.
"Come quick,"
you said.
"He said hi.
He said hi.
He said hi."

GI JOE (to MEL, *also very simple and sweet*)
Your daughter's first word was "Dada."
When she was seven months old.
And then "duck."
And then "book."
She refused to say "Mama" for over a year.

THE TOOTH FAIRY
Hard consonants are easier for babies.
Apparently.

GI JOE
"Not Daddy."
She would call you,
"Not Daddy."

THE TOOTH FAIRY
You bought your son a bike for his second birthday.
But he couldn't reach the pedals until his third birthday.

GI JOE
You bought your daughter a bike when she was twenty-two
    months old.
But she wouldn't go near it until she was thirty-two months
    old.
Then, after five weeks of practice, she could pedal down the
    street.
With her brother.

Jenny Schwartz

THE TOOTH FAIRY
"Look, Ma!
No hands!"

GI JOE
"Look, Ma!
No hands!"

THE TOOTH FAIRY
You bought your kids bike helmets.
And they wore them all the time.
In the house.
In the car.
In the grocery store.
They pretended to be astronauts.
Or pumpkins.

GI JOE (*to* THE TOOTH FAIRY)
Pumpkins were their favorite.

THE TOOTH FAIRY (*to* GI JOE)
They loved to count backwards.

GI JOE (*to* THE TOOTH FAIRY)
They loved to catch crickets.
And let them go.

THE TOOTH FAIRY (*to* GI JOE)
They loved to sing.

GI JOE (*to* MEL)
Your son stuck an action figure behind the wheel of your car.
In the driveway.
You ran it over.
Backing up.

THE TOOTH FAIRY (*to* MEL)

When your daughter was a baby, your son would peer into her
  crib.

On his tippy-toes.

And watch her sleep.

Early one morning, you helped him climb into the crib and lie
  beside her.

You took a picture.

GI JOE (*to* THE TOOTH FAIRY)

She was always taking pictures.

THE TOOTH FAIRY (*to* GI JOE)

Always taking in strays.

GI JOE (*to* THE TOOTH FAIRY)

Always taking little trips.

And excursions.

THE TOOTH FAIRY (*to* GI JOE)

She loved to watch the leaves turn orange and red.

GI JOE (*to* THE TOOTH FAIRY)

Her kids would make piles of leaves and jump in them.

THE TOOTH FAIRY (*to* MEL)

Your daughter's fair.

Like her father.

That's what everyone always says.

She has his eyes.

His skin tone.

And his hair.

And his mild-to-moderate eczema.

And his build.

And his deep disdain for government.

And his spine.

GI JOE *(to* MEL*)*
Your son looked like you.
That's what everyone always said.
You couldn't see it at first.
But then, you could.

THE TOOTH FAIRY
How could you not?

GI JOE
He had your eyes.
Your skin tone.
And your hair.
And your slight lactose intolerance.
And your smile.
And your minor aversion to minivans.
And your guts.

THE TOOTH FAIRY
She has his spine.

GI JOE
He had your guts.

Interlude: Lanie sings a song.

LANIE
> The cat isn't coming back.
> Again.
> She isn't coming back.

> The cat isn't coming back.
> Again.
> She isn't coming back.

Soon, the snow will be melted.
But we won't find anything.
There's nothing under the snow.

The cat isn't coming back.
Again.
She's never coming back.

I love the whole world.
I love the whole world.
I love the whole world.

MEL *is alone.* TED *enters. Very slow. Even more air.*

TED
Did I scare you?

MEL
No.

TED
You jumped.

MEL
Did I?
When?

TED
Just now.
When I walked in.

MEL
I did?
That's funny.
I don't remember jumping.
Are you sure I didn't flinch?

TED
You may have.

MEL
Did I shudder?

TED
You cringed.

MEL
Did I cringe?

TED
You grimaced.

MEL
Did I gasp?

TED
You winced.

MEL
That's funny.
I don't remember wincing.
Was I startled?

TED
You were awake.

MEL
Was I in shock?

TED
You were in pain.

MEL
Was I in physical pain or emotional pain?

TED
Both.

MEL
Shut up.

TED
You asked.

MEL
Shut up.

TED
You asked.

MEL
Shut up.

TED
You asked.

MEL
That's funny.
I don't remember asking.
Was I like this?

She wails. Long and loud.

TED
Hardly.

MEL
Like this?

She wails again. Longer and louder.

TED
Not at all.
It was nothing.
It was subtle.
Just a flash of pain.
Panic.
A pang of grief.
Anguish.
A twinge of agony.
Despair.
And then . . .

MEL
And then?

TED
A glimmer of hope.

MEL
A glimmer of what?

TED
And then . . .

MEL
And then?

TED
Normal.

MEL
Are you there?

TED
I'm here.

MEL
I thought I lost you.

Interlude: GI Joe and the tooth fairy sing a lullaby.

Quietly. As if they are singing the world to sleep.

GI JOE AND THE TOOTH FAIRY
> *I like a room where the blinds all close.*
> *Dark in the morning.*
> *Dark in the evening.*
>
> *I like the lawn underneath my toes.*
> *Cover the garden.*
> *Cover it gently.*
>
> *Tell me a story.*
> *Tell me a story.*
> *Tell me then fly away.*
>
> *I like a child who never grows.*
> *Sleep through the morning.*
> *Sleep through the evening.*
> *Sleep through the morning.*
> *Sleep through the evening.*

THE TOOTH FAIRY *puts money under* LANIE'*s pillow.*

THE TOOTH FAIRY
I should get going.
I'm going to be late.
Next stop Beirut.
They have teeth there too.
But not as many.
No fluoride in the water.

GI JOE
Mind if I join you?

THE TOOTH FAIRY
Not if I join you first.

THE TOOTH FAIRY *and* GI JOE *disappear.*

As the lights fade . . .

TED *(as if in bed)*
Are you sleeping?

MEL *(as if in bed)*
Not yet.
Are you warm enough?

TED
I'm fine.

MEL
I'm thirsty.
I'm thirsty, but I'm lazy.

TED *laughs.*

What's so funny?

TED
I'll get you some water.

MEL
I can get it.

TED
I don't mind.
I'm thirsty too.

Do you want ice?
Mel?

Do you want ice?
Mel?

Are you sleeping?
You're sleeping.
That was quick.

End of play.

Jenny Schwartz

Printed in the USA
CPSIA information can be obtained
at www.ICGtesting.com
LVHW091145150724
785511LV00005B/552